Dharmendra is an excellent trainer!

Satya Raghavan

Director, YouTube Content Partnerships,

Google

Mumbai, India

Dharmendra is the man to learn from!

Jack Canfield

"The Secret" Teacher & Co Creator

of The Chicken Soup

For The Soul Series (Sold 500 Million Copies)

USA

Dharmendra Rai is a genius!

Tony Buzan
Nobel Nominee & Mind Map Inventor
UK

I attended a session by Dharmendra; absolutely fascinating- very precise and hard hitting; I came in attend for only for the initial part and got sucked in and stayed for the entire program; a must for people across levels

Kapil Singhal
Managing Director and India Credit Head
KKR & Co. Inc.
Mumbai , India

Dharmendra's seminar was extensive & enriching

LearningMate

Jolvin Rodrigues
Co-Founder / Global HR Head
LearningMate
Mumbai, India

Dharmendra is a great orator, brilliant
communicator, and an effective instructor

Sharik Currimbhoy
COO
Shahnaz Herbal Group
USA

About The Author

Dharmendra Rai (www.DharmendraRai.com) is an Internationally Acclaimed Brain Literacy Pioneer, Trainer & Author . He specializes in Invisible Selling , Mind Mapping & Brutal Productivity

He has conducted trainings for Executives of Many Fortune 500 Cos & other giant companies like Amazon , Google, Linkedin , Adobe , Unilever , Nestle , Kraft Heinz , Johnson & Johnson , PriceWaterHouse Coopers , KPMG , American Express , NSE , BSE , ISRO , RIL (Reliance Industries) , Reliance Retail, Reliance Nippon Life Insurance , Future Group , ShopClues , IBM , HP , NTT Netmagic , Datamatics , Mphasis , LearningMate , Sapient , Standard Chartered Bank , J P Morgan , Royal Bank of Scotland , Natwest Markets , MasterCard , ICICI Bank , HDFC Bank , SBI , RBI , Exim Bank , Volkswagen , Tata Motors , Cars24 ,

Gyproc (Part of Saint Gobain) , Larsen &
Toubro (L & T) , Grindwell Norton , Atlas Copco
, Thyssen Krupp , Hager , Biocon , Prudential
ICICI Life Insurance , Future Generali Insurance ,
Templeton Mutual Fund , BlackRock Mutual Fund
, SBI Mutual Fund , Mahindra Mutual Fund ,
Airtel , Tata Communications , CNBC, Mudra ,
Publicis Sapient , Dentsu Aegis Network ,
Posterscope , Ambient OOH , Hyperspace ,
InDeed , Nvidia , Rustomjee Builders, Lodha ,
Kanakia , Sun Pharma , Naukri.com , Nykaa , &
for IIT, IIM, Harvard Business School , Wharton
Business School , Johns Hopkins , Oxford ,
London School of Economics (LSE) & CFA
Institute Alumni & Organisations like YPO ,
Young Indians - Yi , CII , ISRO , World HRD
Congress , SHRM , WEF & WIT . Conducted
training & coaching for people in USA , Dubai ,
Singapore, Oman & Indonesia

Dharmendra Rai has appeared in prominent
media like Forbes , Times Of India (TOI) ,

CNBC , Hindustan Times (HT) , BTVi , BloombergQuint , BW BusinessWorld , DNA , Business Standard , Zee Business , Mid Day , Channel V , LiveMint (Ex Wall Street Journal Collab) , MoneyControl , News18 , Business Standard (BS) , Yahoo News , Firstpost , ANI News , DigPu , Dailyhunt , The Sindhian & AIR (All India Radio)

He has 25 Years Work Experience in Training , Sales & Marketing with Companies like Xerox , Morgan Stanley, Alliance Capital (Owned by AXA at the time) & Karvy (Jardine Fleming was a big investor at the time) . Last Position - National Sales Head , Benchmark Mutual Fund (Started by Merrill Lynch Alumna - Taken over by Goldman Sachs) Considered to be a pioneer of Mutual Funds in India

Dharmendra Rai joined the elite list of extremely rare human beings in the history of planet earth , that have been A TED x Speaker Not Just Once

But 5 TIMES

Was interviewed for The World's First Podcast on Mind Mapping & Brain Literacy on YouTube , Apple iTunes , Apple Podcasts , Google Podcasts , Google Music , Spotify , PodBean , PodTail , HubHopper , iHeart , TuneIn , CastBox , RadioPublic & Stitcher . The series has reached listeners in 28 countries

Won the Kotler Award in 2020
Won a UN Award for Brain Literacy in 2019

Did you know ...

... research says people

- eat less food when they use smaller plates ?

- give bigger tips if the tray with the check has a
credit card logo ?

- vote more conservatively at a booth in a church
rather than in a school ? *

Yes that is how counterintuitive the human brain
is!

Whether you are a Fortune 500 executive , a
startup or an independent professional you will ...

... get loads of such insights in this book that will
make you richer , sell better , get promoted
faster & become generally wiser

Dedicated to

The following geniuses whose work has been like a vision enhancing surgery for me . Without them I would still be stumbling in the dark about how the human brain actually works :

Milton H Erickson – The Genius American Psychiatrist and Psychologist who produced almost supernatural results in medical hypnosis and family therapy

Daniel Kahneman & Amos Tversky – Nobel Prize winners for Behavioral Economics . Best known for their path breaking book – Thinking Fast & Slow

Dan Ariely – Probably the most famous Behavioural Economist alive & Author of the amazingly engaging book - Predictably Irrational

Richard Thaler - Nobel Prize winner for Behavioral Economics & the author of the awesome book – Nudge

Bob Cialdini – The Godfather of Influence. Author of the pioneering book – Influence – The Psychology Of Persuasion

Steve Martin & Noah Goldstein – Co authors of the extremely useful book on influence - The Small Big along with Bob Cialdini

* The 3 examples right at the beginning of this book have their origins in The Small Big

Acknowledgments

Chetna Teckchandani – My good friend & eminent graphologist from The UK , for partnering with me to make the World's First Invisible Selling Web Series (More details about that later)

Deepak Malhotra , Durga Arts - My good friend, for helping me massively in designing & printing all my books including this one

Mehul Chimthankar – My good friend & ace photographer for the excellent picture on the back cover

Why has this book been written ?

This book has been written to make you understand the concepts of Invisible Selling as simply & as entertainingly as possible , so that you can immediately implement these strategies & become richer mentally & financially
Most books in the world are written to cure insomnia . This one is to cure inaction

Most books just drone on & on till you feel like tearing your hair & blurting out " Is there a point here ? "
Most books use simplistic statements like " Focus on what you want & not on what you don't want " or " To really become rich you need to know how to earn money " which are silly & don't tell you exactly what to do .

This book is different - it holds your hand from concepts to last miles

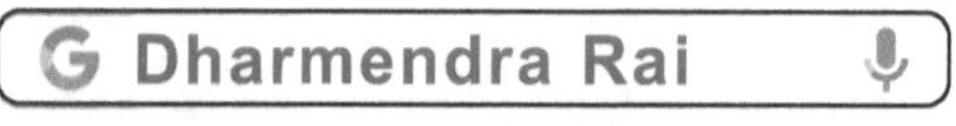

13

Lots of white space has deliberately been used to classify information , increase focus & avoid information overload

Superman Vs General Zod

Invisible Selling is like a superpower . It can be used as Superman or as General Zod. I request you to use it like Superman & not like Zod . Also the understanding of it will protect you from people who use these powerful strategies to hijack your rational brain & sell useless products to you or influence you in a harmful way

Hence deploy ethically & protect smartly

Why Traditional Economics Sucks !

Traditional economics assumes that every human being has a super computer between his ears , knows everything , analyzes everything & decides logically . No human being works that way Imagine this . A man goes to buy tea in a superstore . Traditional economics assumes that he knows about all the brands of tea , their prices, their quality et al & then decides which brand he wants to buy . Nobody has the time , energy & money to do all that . A person may just buy his favourite brand or a new brand for variety or a brand that he 's seen recently in an ad or a brand that 's on discount et al.

Hence traditional economics is pretty lousy at understanding how people actually make decisions

What is Invisible Selling ?

Invisible Selling is a bunch of research backed strategies that can be used for selling or to influence people in a way where

- they don't know that they are being influenced
or
- they know that you re trying to sell them something but they don't resist you because you are not hard selling them or making their brains numb with facts & figures

Most people including senior sales & marketing professionals in Fortune 500 companies do not know much about the latest evidence based sales strategies because

- they have no time to read books(I 'm predicting they will read mine because its fun & easy to read)

- they don't get enough of the right type of training . Most trainers are either into fluffy motivational stuff or have the communication skills of Manmohan Singh

Invisible Selling is very powerful whether you are B2C or B2B selling , online or offline & it is geography & culture agnostic

Invisible Selling can be implemented at a very low cost or for free . That is critical in a world full of fake " digital marketing consultants" who brainlessly advise you on SEO & Google Adwords which can make you bankrupt before you see a single buck in your bank
Invisible Selling is derived from Behavioural Economics , Ericksonian hypnosis , cognitive psychology , social psychology , neuroscience , the science of influence , traditional psychology , NLP et al

Barriers To Effective Implementation Of Invisible Selling Strategies

Most people thinking marketing & selling is " common sense " – the most dangerous words in the English language . There is nothing common sensical about selling . If that were the case everybody would be a billionaire . Selling is very difficult , very counterintuitive & is much more scientific than most people think

Here are 6 things that make most people take selling lightly If you take selling very seriously you literally have an advantage over 99 % of the people on this planet

1) Domain Knowledge

Most people are under the impression that if they know about a subject or an industry they don't need to understand Invisible Selling By that logic the guy with the best memory in an industry should be the most successful person in that industry – never happens

2) Experience

People boast about their experience to prove their credentials This is ironical . People's brains have changed & are changing everyday (& in some ways have remain unchanged for millions of years) . Their ways of finding out information or buying products keeps changing at a blistering pace . Hence experience may be a big liability

3) Intelligence

People having a high IQ tend to be good only at certain types of thinking . Invisible Selling is so non linear that people with a high IQ cannot just stumble upon Invisible Selling They have to study it . Also most people in the world are not as smart as they or their peers think This is known as the Dunning Kruger effect.

Once a man robbed two banks in broad daylight
without a mask or a disguise . Obviously he was
arrested soon

He was shocked when he saw himself on
surveillance tapes & said "But I wore the juice !"
Hold your breath !
He thought rubbing lemon juice on his skin would
make him invisible ! Because lemon juice is used
in invisible ink , he thought he would become Mr
India after rubbing it on himself !

The man - McArthur Wheeler - was not crazy or
on drugs—just terribly wrong
Psychologists David Dunning , Cornell University
& his student Justin Kruger , after researching
plenty of such occurrences , concluded that most
people think very highly about their abilities even
if they are not too bright . This "illusion of
confidence" is now a well documented cognitive
bias called the "Dunning-Kruger effect,"

4) Intuition

Plenty of people take great pride in their intuition & fail badly . Most of the best decisions in the word have been counter intuitive

5) Success

Past success is not just not a guarantee of future success it is a strong indicator of future failure because success builds ego & a know it all approach which can be fatal

6) Anecdotes

Bookstores are full of books which promise you 7 ways to business success or how some lucky guy made a million Dollars Most of them are full of exciting stories . These books are entertaining but also highly harmful . Just because a strategy worked for one man it does 'nt mean that it is a sound strategy

Who Is This Book For ?

This book is for everybody . Because every human is selling something virtually every moment of his life

A man is selling his attractiveness to a woman & vice versa

A parent is selling the concept of hard work & healthy eating to his children
A child is selling the concept of more pocket money to his parent

A CEO is selling the concept of stretching human potential to his team
His team is selling the concept of higher salaries to the CEO

A Fortune 500 CEO is selling the concept of disruption to his board members
His board members are selling the concept of

shareholder value to him

So don't think this book is only for sales &
marketing professionals They will definitely
benefit but so will everyone else

If this book is for everybody why is the focus on business ?

Because ...

a) Business examples can be easily understood by everyone & are interesting because people can relate to popular brands & companies very well

b) Results in business are driven by money . Money is an objective barometer for success & hence a more solid way of understanding how powerful a strategy is . Subjective examples are less powerful & memorable

Why Are People Doomed Without Invisible Selling ?

Without invisible selling companies will perish & individuals would fail horribly The smartest companies in the world like Google , Apple , Facebook & Amazon are already taking Invisible Selling very seriously . Invisible Selling is a virtual superpower All other things remaining equal the man or company that does not know invisible selling is on the path of inevitable suicide

How Should You Read This Book ?

Most people pick up a book without any clear objective .

That is why most of them don't finish reading that book .

Most that finish reading a book don't understand it .

Most that understand – don't remember .

Most that remember – don't implement !

& hence most book buyers are just wasting their time !

So I suggest these 2 objectives be very clear in your mind when you are reading this book

1) Understand the concept very clearly
I have made it as simple & fun as possible If you still have doubts send me a message through my website www.DharmendraRai.com (" OK Google

" " Dharmendra Rai ") I shall do my best to respond

2) Once you have understood the concept , think how you can implement it in your life or business. Think of this in 2 ways

a) How can you make it part of your SOP (Standard Operating Procedure) so every prospect can be exposed to it & everyone in your team can use it &

b) Keep your eyes & ears open to improvise with a strategy , when you are interacting with a prospect

3) Take it once concept at a time Implement & fine tune one concept , get thoroughly grounded in it before moving on to the next concept

There are a total of 5 powerful concepts in this book

4) Keep a notepad & a pen by your side before starting . Do all the quizzes sincerely . That will lead to active & powerful learning. This is proved by cognitive Pshychologists

5) All these concepts are tried & tested So banish scepticism while you are reading it the first time & focus on the top 2 priorities ie understanding & implementing the concepts . Later ,whenever you get time & you want to feed your scepticism ,you can do all the research you want . If you are merely going to use your intuition to be skeptical you will be just wasting your time because all these concepts in their entirety from beginning to last mile are counter intuitive

Why Dharmendra Rai ?

The best guide is one

a) who can give you the science & the facts and figures behind a concept

b) make it fun & simple &

c) has achieved a lot by using the concepts himself so he can give you live examples

If an author is merely a researcher than his book becomes dry & boring

If he is not a researcher & merely a practitioner then he becomes dangerously anecdotal

This is why Dharmendra Rai is probably the best author in the world on this topic . He ticks all 3 boxes in a huge way

Needless to add he is also one of the humblest people on the planet !

CONTENTS

FREE

Chapter

1

FREE

Quiz Alert !

This really happened & is wonderfully detailed in the book Predictably Irrational by Dan Ariely !

Here's the crux of it

Hershey's is a huge non premium chocolate brand . Lindt is a premium chocolate brand

People walked up to a table in a large public building . A sign read " One chocolate per customer " They could choose any one option

The 2 options were

A) Lindt truffles for 15 cents
B) Hershey's Kisses for 1 cent

Write down your estimate of

A) % of people that opted for Lindt

B) % of people that opted for Hersheys

See the answers below

A) Lindt truffles for 15 cent : 73 %

B) Hershey's Kisses for 1 cent : 27 %

Seems to be a rational choice . Most people probably felt that the better quality , aroma , mouth feel, texture , packaging , shape et al justified paying 14 cents more for Lindt

In round 2 both prices were dropped by 1 cent

Hence the options become

A) Lindt truffles for 14 cents

B) Hershey's Kisses for 0 cents

Quiz Alert !

Write down your estimate of
A) % of people that opted for Lindt
B) % of people that opted for Hersheys

See the answers below

A) Lindt truffles for 14 cent : 31 %
B) Hershey's Kisses for 0 cents : 69 %

Isn't that completely irrational ?

Because the difference in the prices has remained the same at 14 Cents ? Logically the percentages should have remained the same !

But most people are not just irrational they are " predictably irrational "
When people are offered something for FREE they become foolish !

I thought of an interesting metaphor . FREE is like a drug called scopolamine

Also called the devil's breath . It is made from seeds of the borrachero tree produced in Columbia

There are numerous stories about how criminals in Colombia use scopolamine to assault victims or rob them(I'm sure Pablo Escobar loved it)

They are blown into the victims' faces

The result ?

People become temporary zombies ! With no

control over their actions - they have their bank
accounts emptied, homes robbed, organs stolen,
or raped by street criminals
There are debates about how powerful
scopolamine is but I love the metaphor for 2
reasons .

It drives home the point that the FREE strategy
is extremely powerful in destroying people's
rational brains in the short run & another
opportunity to request you to use it wisely & also
protect yourself from someone using it on you to
harm you

This also probably answers a question in your
mind as to why I am mentioning FREE as a
strategy when it seems to be such an obvious
one

2 reasons

a) To highlight how powerful it is . Most people
may not have thought of it as a nuke

b) If used the wrong way it can burn your
business to the ground. I am going to highlight
exactly how it is to be used

Why Is FREE So Powerful ?

This is because most people suffer from loss aversion. Ie people will do much more to avoid losses than to get profits . And when something is FREE there is no perceived loss

Obviously nothing in the world is FREE . Everything costs either time, energy or money but most people only think of costs in terms of money & hence the steroidal effects of FREE

Beware

You have to be very careful before you implement the FREE strategy or it can blow up in your face

2 precautions

a) Never offer your core product for FREE

This is because of a concept called anchoring . If you offer your core product for FREE people will be reluctant to pay for it next time because they think that FREE once means FREE always . If you are offering a software FREE for a certain amount of data used or for a certain number of days then calrify upfront that it is not FREE in its entirety . Any loose communication could be disastrous

b) When you are giving something for FREE mention the price of that product or service Because otherwise it gets perceived as a cheap or inferior product . Quite intuitive insn't it ?

Here is an example from the book " Yes!: 50 Scientifically Proven Ways to Be Persuasive" by Cialdini , Goldstein & Martin

A pearl bracelet was given for FREE with a liquor bottle
Group A was told about the offer & asked what their estimate of the price of the bracelet was

Group B was not told about the offer. They were just shown the bracelet & asked what their estimate of its price was

People were willing to pay around 35 % less for the pearl bracelet when it was a FREE add on compared to when it was a standalone product

Examples

When Amazon started offering FREE shipping of orders over a certain amount their sales went up dramatically

My first book The Thin Mind Map Book is

available for FREE reading on Amazon :

https://www.thethinmindmapbook.com/ . I think

this has been instrumental in making my book

extremely popular

with a Google search yielding over 54 Million

search results

42

Implementation

Offer something for FREE to all your prospects .
It is much easier & cheaper to offer something
FREE online Eg a FREE ebook (if you have the
rights or its given for FREE by the author anyway
& this strategy gets approved by your lawyer)
Hence it is not necessary the FREE product
originates from you though that would be
preferable
If you are giving a tangible product for FREE
weigh the pros & cons of the costing .Clarins
gives me lots of FREE samples whenever I buy
from them .This I think works very well because I
am excited to get the FREE stuff & if I like them
I might buy those products on my next visit .
Clarins can afford this because it is a luxury
brand with high margins

You can give away FREE apps.
Evernote is one of the best apps I have ever

used . It is FREE upto a certain amount of data consumed . This is a wonderful example of FREE being used . They have 225 million users as of 29th August 2019

FREE video on FREE

You can see a video on the concept of FREE here :
https://www.youtube.com/watch?v=nhN2M9AFdAk&t=15s
(YouTube " Invisible Selling web series Free ")

This is a part of the first Invisible Selling web series in the world . Please look all my comments under the videos . There is a wealth of examples & updates . I am making each video & its comments as big a repository of information about that strategy as possible

Hot Points

(Hot points are a summary & a mention of additional brief points)

The FREE strategy is one of the most powerful Invisible Selling strategies . People literally lose their logical faculty when they hear the word FREE. Be careful when you offer products for FREE . Never offer your core product for FREE Always mention the price of what you are giving away for FREE

One liner

People will do anything for FREE – even pay for it !

Chapter

2

RECIPROCITY

Quiz Alert !

Click the below link

https://www.youtube.com/watch?v=ZABHozLa1s4

(YouTube “ OK Google “ “Edward Jones Ad 2 “)

The man in the tie makes a huge mistake . What was it ?

After jotting down your answer , see the correct answer below

The huge mistake was : He should not have said
" It's not a big deal at all "

Quiz Alert !

What should he have said instead ?

After jotting down your answer , see the correct
answer below

I have conducted almost 150 seminars in
Invisible Selling & quizzed attendees about this .
Most people say he should have said
-You 're welcome
-Anything for you
-Anytime
-Don't mention it

All these answers are wrong ! He should have
said either
-That 's what partners do or
-I am sure you would have done the same for me

Ok I know I am jumping the Glock but I thought
that was a great way to start this chapter

Here is Invisible Selling Strategy # 2 :
Reciprocity

Do as many favours as you can , for as many
people from your target market as you can ,
without going broke

Because most people who receive the favour

would want to do a favour back for you without

even realising it . This increases the chances

that they will do business with you , everything

else being the same

Why is it so powerful ?

This has strong foundations in evolutionary psychology . When we were cavmen, we had to depend on a good number of close relationships to get us out of trouble Imagine you were a caveman & you got injured . You would not have been able to hunt for food or protect yourself from predators & the elements, unless you had these faithful kemo sabes by your side . If someone helped you & you did not help that person back , you would have been ostracized &

would have died quickly

Today the world is a kinder place but you are still better of with a high number of trusted friends than without . The wiring has been reinforced for several millions of years of evolution . Hence it is almost second nature to like the person who does us a favour & be willing to do a favour back for him as an instinct

Examples

Here is an excellent incident mentioned in Bob Cialdini's book Influence The Psychology Of Persuasion

In 1985 Ethiopia was going through a very tough time - the worst famine to hit the country in a century - it left 1.2 million dead . It was also a terrible year for Mexico- it suffered an earthquake ! Inspite of all the pain Ethiopia was going

through it paid Mexico as way of relief aid ! Why would Ethiopia increase its suffering at such a terrible time ? It is because Mexico had come to Ethiopia 's aid in 1935 when it was being invaded by Italy

2 things shouted out at me

a) Ethiopia was reciprocating Mexico's favour done 50 years ago ! (More on elapsed time of favours later)
b) This transaction was between countries & not individuals . This makes the case for reciprocity more compelling than if it were between individuals because decision making by groups is much more complicated than between individuals

Distinctions

Quiz Alert !

In the eyes of a favour giver does the value of a favour increase as time passes or decrease as time passes In other words does that favour behave like wine or bread ?

After jotting down your answer see the correct answer below

You ll be shocked how many people get this wrong

A favour behaves like wine in the eyes of the favour giver

& How does it behave in the eyes of the favour getter

Exactly the opposite !

If you have done a favour to someone, as time passes, the value of the favour will keep increasing in your mind and decreasing in his mind

Quiz Alert !

Now that you know this, what will be your strategy after doing someone a favour ?

After jotting down your answer see the correct answer below

Ask the person to do something for you IMMEDIATELY ! The more you delay the greater the chances of him thinking your favour was a small one or of him forgetting your favour totally ! I know this sounds really mercenary but most people you have done a favour for will not notice the "quid pro quo" nature of your request or won't think negatively about it

What Makes A Great Favour ?

Every favour does'nt need to be a great favour . You may want to reserve great favours for your largest prospects

There are 3 elements that make a great favour according to Bob Cialdini

Significance

This need not be expensive. I train on subjects other than Invisible Selling . One of them is a subject called Mind Mapping I keep giving CEOs

& decision makers who are parents of school going children – books on Mind Mapping for students One of the best ways to win the heart of a parent is to do something for his child ! Not expensive but VERY significant

Unexpectedness

A no brainer really .If you are a private banking client who has a huge amount of money being handled by a wealth manager at a bank, you tend to expect to be called to lavish parties & have interest rates on a business loan to be lower than the rack rate . But if you get something unexpected like an invite to the CEO's house party where you ll get a chance to meet guests like Elon Musk, than that could be a major event in your life

Personalisation

If a client has a complaint against a company & the CEO himself picks up the phone & reassures

him that he'll personally ensure everything is taken care of, then that may be deemed as a favour to the client . Expensive . Use smartly

Implementation

Use every opportunity to do favours to your target market. Use the FREE strategy seriously . Always be on the lookout for ways in which you could do favours to a large number of people – say offering valuable tips on getting more business on social media For big clients you could be on the lookout for giving them things that enhance business like a high networth networking event et al or enhance their image – say a chance to meet a celebrity

Video

See the Invisible Selling web series video on reciprocity
https://www.youtube.com/watch?v=O_iEvC36NCM
(YouTube " Invisible Selling Web Series reciprocity ")

Hot Points

Do favours as often as possible for your target market without going broke
- If he says thank you - nail it in
- if he does not – relax, it does 'nt necessarily mean he does'nt appreciate your favour
- ask for a favour back asap
- if that's not possible , when you ask for it later , remind him of the favour you dit for him. Eg you could ask him how he benefited from your favour or what the outcome of your favour was.
A great favour is one that is
- Unexpected
- Significant
- Personal

One Liner

Want to be a business superman ? Be a favourman !

Chapter

3

SOCIAL PROOF

Quiz Alert !

Imagine you see an infomercial & are inclined to buy the product being sold . The infomercial ends with this call to action line

" Operators are waiting please call now "

How would you rate your likelihood of buying the product on a scale of 1-10 where 1 indicates least likely to buy

After jotting down your answer see the correct answer below

Before the answer - another Quiz Alert !

Now imagine the call to action line changed to

" If operators are busy , please call again "

How would you rate your likelihood of buying the product on a scale of 1-10 where 1 indicates least likely to buy

After jotting down your answer see the correct answer below

You 'll be shocked to know it's the second line that turned out to be infinitely more powerful !

This really happened in a commercial written by Colleen Szot (From the book - Yes : 50 Secrets From The Science of Persuasion by Cialdini , Goldstein & Martin)

How could this happen ? Does'nt the line " If operators are busy , please call again " make people think that this company is plainly apathetic ? If you think so , then this is a good time to appreciate how useless intuition can often be in understanding specifically sales & marketing and generally in understanding human psychology

So what exactly is going on ?

When people hear the line " Operators are waiting please call now " they imagine plenty of

tele executives waiting for their phones to ring .
Not a very exciting picture

When they hear " If operators are busy , please call again " they visualize frantic taking of orders & truckloads of products being shipped " If so many people are buying their product – the reasoning goes – the product must be an excellent one & I want in !

The concept is called Social Proof . It means people copy what other people do or what they think other people are doing

Why Is It So Powerful ?

Because the brain is a very limited organ . It has too much data to handle & keeps searching for shortcuts . Imagine you were a caveman & saw 20 cavemen running in one direction The best course of action for you would have been to just follow them . There could have been 2 scenarios

1) It made sense to run – maybe there's a
predator or an avalanche nearby or
2) Maybe it was a false alarm – no harm done &
a few calories lost

Hence it does make sense to follow the herd
when your downside is nothing But most people
follow the herd even when the downside could be
crippling Eg investing at the height of a stock
market boom, just because everyone from your
Uber driver & your boss is investing

Examples

" Billions and Billions Served " A punchline of
McDonalds clearly uses Social Proof

Google & Amazon ratings influence prople
massively in their purchase decisions

68

Distinctions

People follow people who are like them (or people they aspire to be like) . Hence if you are selling an App that has been bought by Microsoft & you are pitching to a startup – it makes sense to mention the names of startups that have bought your app, in addition to Microsoft . This increases the chances of your sale going through, over merely mentioning Microsoft though having Bill Gates' company as a client may be more impressive

Beware

Beware of " negative social proof "

Eg: People who were told that average electricity consumption by their neighbours was higher than theirs , increased their energy consumption ! (From the book Yes! 50 Secrets From the Science of Persuasion by Cialdini, Goldstein & Martin)

So if you want people to behave in a certain way only show them examples of the behavior that you want the to adapt

Implementation

If the numbers are impressive tell your prospects how many clients you have , show them testimonials , show them pictures of large number of people buying your products et al

Video

See the Invisible Selling webseries on Social Proof :

https://www.youtube.com/watch?v=7HUYt3XNHgM&t=2s

(YouTube " Invisible Selling web series social proof ")

Hot points :

Highlight your number of clients , number of YouTube views on your YouTube channel or number of testimonials you have received

When you talk to a big guy show him big guy testimonials . When you talk to a small guy – show him small guy testimonials

Talk about the behaviour you want people to indulge in – not the behaviour you want them to avoid

One liner

The more clients you have – the more clients you get

Chapter

4

The Zeigarnik Effect

" 2 Rules For Success

#1 : Never Reveal All You Know "

Sticks to your brain like Velcro does'nt it ?

Here's another one

"Heard this BULLSHIT about communication from ignorant trainers ?
Your words communicate 7 % your tone of voice - 38 % & your body language - 55 % Yes it is bullshit !

What is the real story ? Comment " Mind Map" & I ll let you know "

This post of mine on Linkedin attracted over 2,000 comments ! To get the answer see here : https://dharmendraraiblog.com/33-2/

 (OK Google " " Dharmendra Rai Blog " & search for Mehrabian")

The brain is aroused by something unfinished or a mystery & can go without sleep , water & food to get the whole picture ! Explains why suspense stories like those of Sherlock Holmes are so popular . Sherlock himself believed in this when he said "Omne ignotum pro magnifico " Latin for ""everything unknown is in the place of a magnificent thing"

Also explains why people do binge watching of web series leading to Netflix being worth over $ 200 Billion in market capitalisation ! You just have to see how it ends ! Don't you ?

Why is it called the Zeigarnik effect ?

One day, while sitting in a busy Viennese restaurant in the 1920s, Bluma Zeigarnik , a Russian psychologist , was dining at a restaurant . She noticed that the waiters had an excellent memory for unfulfilled orders . As soon an order was fulfilled , that data seemed to vanish from their minds . Logical - as it was no longer deemed important . This observation let Bluma to conduct several experiments that confirmed that this is a widespread phenomenon

Examples

An excellent way this was done by Burger King was to offer people a " Mystery Burger " Eg in France you could pay 2 euros & get a plain white box with a question mark on it . It would contain any one of the fast-food giant's 10 most iconic burger options . This created a huge buzz around the brand

But a man who virtually institutionalized this was Steve Jobs of Apple . He understood The Zeigarnik Effect very well & took it with the utmost seriousness . Apple executives were warned to not reveal new product details to outsiders . They were threatened with severe legal consequences if they failed to keep their mouths ziplocked . Apparently Apple also had spies to follow some people for good measure

So secretive are the new products of Apple under development that there is a gargantuan industry of Apple new product forecasters with blogs , WhatsApp groups , offline hobbyists & Youtubers

The greatest manifestation of Steve 's seriousness about The Zeigarnik Effect was in his product launch talks . if you look at the formats of these talks, they are all about talking about a problem & then showing how the iWhatever solves those problem . So the second he talks about a problem, people are hooked because they are wondering how that problem would be solved & their minds are racing to see

if they can crack it before the answer is revealed
Eg : The iPhone launch .Throughout the talk
people are incredibly eager to see the iPhone .
Steve teases them by saying " I have it right
here in my pocket " & then shows it for split
second making the crowd lust for it even more
.Very much akin to a striptease artist !
 I suggest you see Steve 's iPod talk & iPhone
talk very deeply to observe these points Both
links here for your quick reference

https://www.youtube.com/watch?v=kN0SVBCJqLs
("OK Google " " iPod launch ")

https://www.youtube.com/watch?v=0XJg74qnvxE
(" Ok Google " " iPad launch ")
These 2 in my view are the 2 best product
launches by Steve

Beware

You better live up to the promise !

If you are creating suspense your climax better deliver !

Arnold Schwarzenegger talks about this superbly in his biography Total Recall He talks about the bodybuilder he admired the most – Sergio Oliva . The only bodybuilder Arnold really feared losing his titles to . At the top of any field everyone is talented & hard working . If you want to be # 1 in any field you have to go beyond that & attack people's perceptions & use psychological warfare . Arnold Schwarzenegger, 7 times Mr Olympia & the greatest bodybuilder in the history of the planet , was a genius at that . So to see him praise somebody else for it is fascinating indeed . Sergio would be very secretive about his workouts . At the time of the competitions he would cover his body before he needed to show

it off on stage . Rumours would start several months before that he's really been working out crazily on his biceps or lats or quads et al . So to see him all covered up before the competition would make his competitors lose their cool & they would be mentally defeated even before the competition would start . But as Arnold states – this only worked because Sergio he had an incredibly great body & he worked unbelievably hard . If he did not have substance this strategy would have failed miserably
So fluff may sell or not , It 's better to have substance before using any strategy especially the Zeigarnik Effect because here you are hyping people's expectations

A brilliant way in which Arnold used the Zeigarnik Effect was creating a trailer for his autobiography – Total Recall – probably the only book trailer or the only well marketed & well produced book trailer in the world at that time

You can see it here :

https://www.youtube.com/watch?v=Yd0WkW5tUog
(" OK Google "arnold book trailer ")

Implementation

Keep people guessing . Use quizzes . Tell them about a launch date but not the product . Keep announcing small tit bits about your product so people keep following you to get the full picture

Video

See the Invisible Selling web series on The Zeigarnik Effect
https://www.youtube.com/watch?v=-NqFKojnnHo&fbclid=IwAR09XpvHnAX1hqroYw2awyPcNYOoITJkGIO8kgEbS4-B4imrnDdDdzWa4Xs
(" OK google " " Dharmendra Rai Invisible Selling ZeigarniK ")

Hot Points :

Keep people guessing . Don't offer them all
information at one time This way people chase
you instead of you chasing them
If people are sweating for the climax , make sure
they feel it was worth their while

One Liner

Here's the biggest tip for success. On second
thoughts I'll tell you later

Chapter

5

Anchoring

Quiz Time !

Imagine this or use your memory . You are at a site office of a real estate project . You are warmly greeted by an enthusiastic sales lady . You ask her " Could you show me your offerings ? "

What do you think her response would be ?

After jotting down your answer , see the correct answer below

Hint for you to refine your answer if needed : It is likely to be exactly 4 words long !

Bingo !

The chances are very high that you cracked this because most companies are trained by foolish sales trainers who don't understand brain literacy

The most likely response from her is going to be " What is your budget ? " or a variation of that . The reasoning being – If you have only a certain budget why bother showing you something out of range & wasting time . That is a perilously wrong thought

Now let's do something else & come back to this story later

This is an exercise I do in all my seminars & this is exactly what happens when there are at least

40 people in the room ! In this illustration I have presumed there are exactly 40 people in the room

I request 20 people to leave the room . They are selected in such a way to ensure that a random half are out of the room . It is done through a scientific process . It would not be a very scientific act to just say " All the people in this part of the room are requested to take a walk around the block "

I show the "inside 20" a painting . For good reasons I shall tell you the name of the painting later . Suffice to say it is a painting that looks like its been made by one of the best painters in the world

& I say " Look at the above painting . Grab a pen & paper & write down the answer to these 2 questions in under 10 seconds each

1 : Do you think this painting is worth over Rs 700 Crores or under Rs 700 Crores

2 : If you were as rich as Jeff Bezos , The richest man in the world with a net worth of $ 143 Billion , & you felt like buying this painting how much would you be willing to pay for it ?

After that they are ushered out of the room & the other group of 20 people enters the room

I tell them " Look at the above painting . Grab a pen & paper & write down the answer to these 2 questions in under 10 seconds each

1 : Do you think this painting is worth over Rs 1 Lac Crores or under Rs 1 Lac

2 : If you were as rich as Jeff Bezos , The Richest man in the world with a net worth of $ 143 Billion , & you felt like buying this painting how much would you be willing to pay for it ?

Before I tell you the answers you should understand that these anecdotal stories are only to drive home this knowledge Anecdotal evidence is very tricky when you are trying to prove something .Hence I am using concepts that are proved by the best researchers in the world & using anecdotal evidence & exercises only to drive them deeper in your brain

Back to the painting exercise

Quiz Alert !

What do you think the average of the first group was ?

What do you think the average of the second group was ?

After jotting down your answers , see the correct answers below

I 'm going to go out on a limb & deduce that you estimated the first group's average as higher than that of the second group . That is exactly what happened to the utter shock of everybody in the room !

You are also encouraged to play this quiz with your friends & the chances are that most of them will answer in a similar way

I suggest you think about this in this way . Salesmen A & B try to sell the same product to the same type of client . A knows about this invisible selling strategy & B does not . A manages to sell it at 1000 times the price that B manages to sell it . Ie other things remaining the same, a business can scale its profits up 1000X with just one invisible selling strategy !

Why did this happen ? Why was the first group willing to pay more than the second group for the same product ?

The answer is Anchoring

I would like to define anchoring as practically &
usefully as possible My definition is

The first impression is the last impression

A very old line which is now backed up by very
credible research

Why & how Anchoring works

Most people have no clue what the rational price
of a product should be . They are looking for
some data to make they feel happy about a price
Eg : Imagine Jimmy does'nt have too much
experience buying furniture & needs to buy a
chair. He   visits a furniture showroom . Imagine
the salesperson shows him a chair for Rs 5,000 .
It seems to be a nice chair . It looks nice . He

feels comfortable when he sits in it . It swivels well . But his mind is racing . Should he buy it ? Is it the right price ? Should he check out a few more stores ? Amazon ? If the salesman is trained on invisible selling he may say " In case you are also looking out for a table , here's a nice one for Rs 10,000" & points to a decent looking table . Now what do you think is his state of mind ? Better or worse ? For most people in Jimmy's situation it would be better because now his brain is thinking it is doing something rational . The table is bigger than the chair & the hence it is only logical that the chair be cheaper than the table . In other words his brain was looking for an anchor , a context , a refence point for him to justify paying Rs 5,000 for the chair & it found it . In his desperation to find a straw to grasp he overlooked the possibility that Rs 10,000 may not have been a rational price for the table in the first place & hence his whole reasoning may have been wrong . Most people don't have the thinking skills or time to deep dive about this A similar thing happened when people were asked to decide how much they would be willing to pay for the painting . Unless they worked for Southeby's or Christie's or were art aficionados , their mind was going through its' memory files to find an answer. Maybe they read something about a painting being sold ? Maybe there was something about an extravagant painting in a James Bond movie ? Chances are they drew a blank & in their desperation latched on to the LAST figure they had in mind - Rs 700 Crores for some & Rs 1 Lac for some .

Completely irrational ? Welcome to the human brain !

The name of the painting is The Massacre of the Innocents by Peter Paul Rubens

It was sold by Sotheby's on July 10, 2002 for over C$100 million, to Canadian businessman and art collector Kenneth Thomson, 2nd Baron Thomson of Fleet . I cannot reproduce it here for copyright reasons

Implementation

Always talk about a high number while talking about pricing because the first number that enters the client's mind is critical – it's the anchor

Now let us go back to the real estate example

Quiz Alert !

You know what a poorly trained sales lady would say if she was asked " Could you show me what you have on offer ? " by a prospect

Now imaging you are the sales rep at the site office . You have just been given a superpower – a concept called anchoring . You were Bruce Banner & now you are The Hulk . Unleash your powers ! You are asked this common question by a prospect " Could you show me what you have on offer ? " How would you respond ?

 After jotting down your answer see the correct answer below

The best answer would be to suggest the prospect see a sample flat . And show him the most expensive flat . If you had a flat that costs Rs 100 Crores, that would be excellent . If you didn't have one, you should start offering one . He may not be interested in buying a flat worth Rs 100 Crores He may have been looking at buying a flat worth Rs 20 Crores After seeing the Rs 100 Crores flat, he may be willing to fork out Rs 50 Crores or Rs 40 Crores or maybe Rs 25 Crores for another flat that suits his pocket & choice . There is no guarantee of this happening but the probability of anchoring working is very high . Imagine the steep increase in profits for the real estate company that uses this strategy . I have done invisible selling seminars for over 100 real estate companies in India People who have used it have been thrilled at the rise in their income of this virtually risk free strategy

Some of my seminar participants had expressed reservations about clients budgets being very strict & the fear of them walking away . That is very unlikely to happen because he has invested time , energy & money in a site visit & will certainly ask for more options instead of just flying off. Also most budgets are "fudgets". Forgotten in a second when attractive product is sighted.

I have used real estate as an example because plenty of people can relate to it . Bears repetition - all Invisible Selling strategies can be used in any industry

Hence Anchoring also solves a major dilemma in sales people's minds about whether they should reveal their price first or wait for the prospect to mention his budget . It is obvious from what we have learnt about Anchoring that as a salesman you should shoot first . It is suicide to let the prospect go first because the power of anchoring that was in your hands in now being relinquished to the prospect . Suppose you wanted to sell a suite of services to a prospect for Rs 10 Lacs & instead of suggesting you have a product for Rs 10 Lacs , you ask the client about his budget & he says Rs 5 Lacs . His real budget is likely to be much higher (When have you ever revealed your true budget when you have been asked this silly question) . Now he has already anchored the prospective price he will pay for your product at Rs 5 Lacs & is unlikely to pay you Rs 10 Lacs even if he finds it to be a worthwhile buy & has the budget for it

Behavioral Economics consultant Steve Martin has analyzed a set of companies that have been sold . Here are the results

Companies sold where the seller mentioned his asking price ie used anchoring , resulted in an average sales price of $ 24 . 8 Million (Rs 174 Crores)

Companies where prospective buyers were asked what price they would be willing to pay for companies being offered to them ie not using anchoring , resulted in an average sales price of $ 19 .7 Million (Rs 140 Crores)
Conclusion

The sellers who did not understand anchoring were poorer by an average of Rs 35 Crores !

I think the real reason for the failure of the Tata Nano was the failure of understanding the concept of anchoring . Think about the first time you heard about the Nano car . What was the most prominent thing that shouted out at you ! Bingo ! The price tag ! It was supposed to cost Rs 1 Lac ! So that price got anchored into the minds of people . An initial batch of card was sold for Rs 1 Lac. All cars after that were priced higher than Rs 1 Lac . If pricing it at Rs 1 Lac was not viable then there were 2 options a) Reduce the cost & sell it for Rs 1 Lac or b) Kill the Nano brand & create a new brand . Since neither was done Tata Motors bore heavy losses on the Nano brand & it was eventually dropped

Some questions you may have in your mind

How can you use anchoring if you don't have an expensive product ?
Create an expensive product . If that product sells – the revenue will be a bonus If it does 'nt sell it 'll pull up the revenue of your other products

Eg : A Samsung Galaxy S20 Ultra mobile phone costs
Rs. 92,999 on Amazon in India on 15 th June 2020 . It is doubtful there would be too many

takers but it sure makes other Samsung phones appear to be a bargain Also it positions Samsung as a technology leader with dazzling tech as used in the S 20

How can I use Anchoring when I sell a commodity product ?

Never sell a commodity . Create a brand out of a commodity . That is what Starbucks & McDonalds have done

Hot Points

- The first number in the mind of the prospect is Critical
- Be careful with the upper range. It should sound real
Always have a super expensive product that looks like a Trillion Dollars

One Liner

Without anchoring you'll be adrift

The Book Ends But Learning Never Ends

Keep sharpening your Invisible Selling skills &
keep adding new arrows to your quiver with
these FREE resources

- The Invisible Selling Web Series of 52 episodes
is an exhaustive compendium of strategies
You can access it here :

https://www.youtube.com/watch?v=h7xxzhraqMA
(YouTube " Invisible Selling Web Series 1)

- The World's First TEDx Talk on Invisible Selling
:
https://www.youtube.com/watch?v=vfBW-
gFK0wg&t=47s
(YouTube " Invisible Selling TEDx)

- My blog which is packed with articles on
Invisible Selling :
https://dharmendraraiblog.com/
(Google " Dharmendra Rai Blog)
Follow me on LinkedIn & Facebook by searching
for " Dharmendra Rai "
Want Dharmendra Rai to train your team on

Invisible Selling ?

Want to become a Certified Invisible Selling Trainer & train others to realize their full potential?

Want to get certified as a Invisible Selling expert online?

Want to attend a public seminar on Invisible Selling?

Want Dharmendra Rai to be a keynote speaker at your next event?

For all the above and for any query related to Mind Maps, Memory, Creativity, Learning, Productivity & Invisible Selling, please message me through my website

Happy Invisible Selling !